AN INTRUDER, A WITNESS &

God's Divine Plan!

D1203282

SHELENA A. HICKMAN

An *Intruder*, A *Witness* & God's Divine *Plan*!

Copyright 2023© Shelena A. Hickman

ISBN # 979-8-218-19835-0

Author: Shelena A. Hickman

Editor: Valerie L. McDowell

Interior Book Design: Velin@Perseus-Design.com

Cover Design: danny_media

Publisher: Power2Excel Agency, LLC

What Others Have To Say...

If you want to know how to live boldly with confidence after opposition, this is the book for you. Life brings joy and pain. We would literally fall without the hand of God carrying us through. Shelena will capture your heart as she shares her story. Her determination and passion for the Lord is the spiritual conduit we need to survive after opposition.

-Sheryl Woods

This book is about hope. Where in God, nothing is so damaged or lost that He cannot heal or restore it. It lets you see the victory we have in God through His Son, Jesus Christ. Shelena paints a picture of life that many can identify with in their own sufferings and trials of life as a believer or non-believer. But God!!!

-Pastor Anita Williams

Shelena is a jewel in our lives. We are fortunate to have her as a wonderful and delightful niece. You will see an example of Shelena's faith and endurance exemplified as you read this book. She is God's gift to us.

-Uncle Henry & Aunt Von

Dedication

This book is dedicated to my mother,

Yolande Guide.

The strongest woman I know!

Contents

Introduction

I have always known that someone more extraordinary and significant than my mom and dad had a plan for my life. I just didn't know who it was. There was always a resounding voice that would give me sound advice and direction. Because I never saw God, I assumed I was listening to my subconscious speak back to me. But as I grew older and gave my life to Jesus, I found out that the inner-knowing and unctions (direct guidance to move) I had were from my Heavenly Father above. So, when I needed guidance, my foundation was the Word of God, and specifically the scripture found in Jeremiah 29:11 (TLB),

> *"For I know the plans that I have for you, says the Lord. They are plans for good and not for evil, to give you a future and a hope."*

It is my spiritual GPS and always gets my attention. If I hadn't known the power of this scripture, the events that took place in my life would not have been as favorable!

* * *

Growing up young and naïve in Trinidad, West Indies, in the mid-1970s, my parents, while in their early 20's and with no real direction, became involved with one another. Unfortunately, they had a rocky start to their relationship and were influenced by negative family interferences contributing to their dysfunction. On top of that, the difficulty is even greater when the mother of the man you are involved with wants nothing to do with you, especially when you are not married.

My mother experienced this rejection from the beginning when she found out she was pregnant with her first child, my brother, Sheldon. After a difficult birth, my father's mother (my grandmother) initially took him away from her for her to recuperate. However, my mother was deprived of the joy of loving and caring for her first child because my father's mother was very controlling. She often would come to the house, take Sheldon from my mother without notice, and raise him for months at a time. This further traumatized my mother in caring for her son. However, despite this interference, and as unimaginable as this sounds, my mother and father got together again, and she became pregnant with me, a girl.

Throughout the pregnancy, my mother experienced continuous oppression and was worn down by frequent bouts of depression and anxiety. In addition, before my birth, and to further try and hinder the plan of God for my life, my father's mother (my grandmother) convinced him to force my mother to abort me. He gave her $20 and a bottle of pills to go and see a doctor. When my mother visited the local doctor, he refused the procedure! The Great Physician and this local physician protected me from the womb. God's plan for my life would prevail, and no one, not even my family, could thwart it. God's Word was already being manifested through some scriptures I now hold dear. Psalms 139:13-14 (NKJV),

> *For you formed my inward parts; You covered me in my mother's womb. I will praise You, for I am fearfully and wonderfully made.*

and Isaiah 54:17 (NKJV),

> *No weapon formed against you shall prosper, and every tongue which rises against you in judgment You shall condemn.*

Looking back, I can see that although my beginning was turbulent, my mother and father were the vehicles God used to get me here.

As time passed, God's providence for my life slowly unfolded through the obedience of my other grandmother, my mother's mother, Lucy Guide. We called her Granny. Granny was born in Trinidad but was living in St. Croix, U.S. Virgin Islands, and felt compelled to get me to the United States to become a citizen. My mother was living in Trinidad then. So, Granny sent a plane ticket for my mom to leave Trinidad and come to St. Croix. At seven months pregnant with me, my mother boarded a plane and flew to a destination that would open so many doors for my future life.

> My mother and father were the vehicles God used to get me here.

This new life was short-lived after about a year. My mother longed to be reunited with her firstborn, her only son, Sheldon, whom she was forced to leave behind. Therefore, she decided to return to Trinidad with me after I turned one, hoping to reunite with my brother, who was now about two years of age.

This move would become a very dark time for my mother, filled with emotional and physical abuse. For the first seven years of my life, my strongest memories were of the violence in our household. Fortunately, my greatest enjoyment came when my mother dropped me off to stay with my great-grandmother, Ma-Ruby Senhouse. Being with her was a refreshing escape because she was a *great* grandmother. She made me feel loved and safe. I never wanted to leave her, but I often went back and forth between her house and my mother's because I also missed my mother so much. This period of my life would usher in the next season.

Ecclesiastes 3:1 (KJV) says that,

> *to every thing there is a season, and a time to every purpose under the heaven.*

Some years later, Granny Lucy would be used again to get me to God's appointed destination for my life. I learned that the rejection of one grandmother did not prevail because the love and prayers of another grandmother covered me from my natural birth.

* * *

Boarding a plane from Baytown, Texas, my granny flew to Trinidad, West Indies, to get me. I was sitting on the house steps when I saw my grandmother's face. Although I did not know who she was, I told myself I was leaving with that woman because she looked like someone I could trust. She appeared as an angel in her lemon-colored dress on that summer day. My grandmother walked through the house gates and met with my dad. She told him with boldness that she was not leaving without me! My grandmother's obedience in listening to the Spirit of the Lord concerning me allowed the prophetic moves of God to work both in Trinidad and Texas. So, at the tender age of eight, I began a new life in Baytown, Texas, with the love of God flowing through my grandparents, Alfred and Lucy Guide. They both took the time to restore me, the broken and confused child, to normalcy.

> *Before I made you in your mother's womb, I chose you. Before you were born, I set you apart for a special work. I appointed you as a prophet to the nations.* Jeremiah 1:5 (NCV).

By this time, my mother and father were no longer together. My dad would later marry, but my mother struggled with moving on due to the trauma of their past involvement. Yet, although my mother did not have any successful relationships with the fathers of her children, the Lord blessed her with three girls and one boy. My brother Sheldon was the oldest; I was the oldest girl; and then my two younger sisters, Sherene and Sharleen, made our family connection complete. Finally, with the help of Granny Lucy once more, the Lord made way for all of us to move to Baytown, Texas. I cannot express how happy and overjoyed I was to have my mother back. I was also excited that I had my siblings to play with now.

As an immigrant to the U.S., my mother was here on a permanent VISA. With little to no experience, she had to work odd jobs at fast-food restaurants at various hours during the day and night to make a living while we stayed with our grandmother. Mother continued to perform these jobs until she was approved for housing. My siblings and I stayed with our mother off and on, attending different schools over the years while she worked to gain stability. Fortunately, Granny always welcomed us to her home and loved having us around.

Life remained challenging, but the years flew by. Finally, after graduating high school, I approached a fork in the road for my next steps. Unfortunately, I didn't know which way to go. Because I lacked spiritual guidance, I was unaware that the true direction I needed in my life was a stable relationship with God, my Heavenly Father.

Years later, my mother sought an opportunity to better her life and enrolled in the local community college down the street from Granny Lucy's house. She worked hard and persevered, earning a Certified Nurse's Assistant Certificate. Even though my mother now had a better job, she continued to work long hours assisting the elderly. Additionally, even with the better pay, our family was not getting ahead. I thought going off to college myself would help. I signed up, intending to pursue becoming an accountant, although I never really liked the subject. I also didn't have a driver's license, and there certainly was no money to buy a car.

Not having what I considered necessary material things others had at home caused me to develop low self-esteem. I felt especially insecure as I looked at girls my age and the things they had. This created a lack of confidence, and I started looking to others to affirm me because I always doubted that I could do things independently. I often would say I couldn't do something before I even tried. In my head, I had convinced myself not to try because I esteemed others higher and automatically thought they could do it better.

Around this time, my brother, Sheldon, started attending church services with my mother and gave his life to Jesus Christ. I knew there was something different about him, but I couldn't put my finger on it. I now know that it was the love of God inside of him, drawing me closer to him. He had changed, and I could see the metamorphic transformation in his speech, outer appearance, and attitude. I wanted the peace and joy he seemed to have all the time now. So, one day while he was leaving with his Bible, I grabbed my things and quickly followed him and my mother to Bible study.

After attending church with them a few times, I realized I needed a Savior! Every time I participated in a service, the preacher seemed to knowingly preach about the sin I was in or knew how I was feeling. It was exhausting, always feeling empty and worthless inside and unworthy of God's love. I didn't know how to make myself perfect, and it was causing me a lot of unnecessary stress. I was trying to clean myself up to come to the Lord when all He wanted me to do was, come! Just as I was. The Lord was drawing me to Him with all my failures, anger, and mistakes. Finally, one Sunday morning, my eyes, ears, and heart were receptive to the Word of God. I got out of my seat and came down the aisle crying and asking for forgiveness from God for everything I had ever done. I confessed every sin I could think of and asked forgiveness for the ones I could not remember. Redeemed, I stood before the altar and surrendered my life to the Lord completely, unashamed. I felt lighter than a feather and cleaner than a fresh shower!

Looking back, I can see how God used my brother to draw me into a relationship with Him. From that day forward, my brother would read the Word of God with me, and we would share our testimonies of how God made a way for us that day! It was a beautiful bond we shared, and I thank God for my brother taking the time to mentor me spiritually. There are many truths and scriptures that I hold on to today because Sheldon sowed his heart and zeal for the Word of God into me. And for this, I am extremely and forever grateful. His passion for learning about God shaped my early spiritual walk. My favorite scripture he shared with me was Mark 11:22-24 (NKJV),

> So Jesus answered and said to them, "Have faith in God. For assuredly, I say to you, whoever says to this mountain, 'Be removed and be cast into the sea,' and does not doubt in his heart, but believes that those things he says will be done, he will have whatever he says. Therefore I say to you, whatever things you ask when you pray, believe that you receive them, and you will have them.

Tragically, six months after experiencing this tremendous high, one Sunday morning, my family's life drastically changed in the blink of an eye! I remember my Uncle Henry pulling on my toe and shaking me to wake up because I had to go and see my mother. I was cranky and didn't want to wake up. Finally, when he wouldn't stop pulling on my toe, I decided to sit up on the bed. My uncle then sat beside me, and I could immediately tell he had been crying. This is when he took a deep breath and told me my brother was involved in an accident. Before he could get the rest out, I suggested we go see him at the hospital. My uncle then stated we couldn't do that because he was dead. When I heard those words, my insides became numb, and my mind went into shock. All kinds of emotions and thoughts were running through my head, but I couldn't think about myself.

I needed to get to my family. I had to be there for my mother and my sisters. I put my feelings aside and leaned on the Lord to strengthen me in our dire hour of need. After living a sold-out life serving God, Sheldon was promoted to his Heavenly Father at 23 years old. He was the last car in a 4-car pile-up hit from behind. He was killed on impact with a blow to the head. He had left early that morning to minister to a young man who was incarcerated but never returned home.

I believe Sheldon walked closely with the Lord daily, and the Lord made him an offer he couldn't refuse as he did Enoch in the Bible.

In Matthew Henry's commentary on Enoch, the 7th person born on the earth from Adam, he notes, "God often takes those soonest whom he loves best; the time they lose on earth is gained in heaven, to their unspeakable advantage." The Bible doesn't say Enoch died; it just says, "he was not, for God took him." He was not any longer in this world; he

9

was changed, as the saints shall be, who are alive at Christ's second coming.[1]

The day my brother was buried, I asked the Lord to allow me to carry on the mantle of his anointing as I wanted to be a strong witness as he was. The Lord honored my request. And since that day, I've been running for Jesus with every fiber of my being. With the Lord's help, I can live out the scripture in Philippians 3:14 (KJV),

I press toward the mark for the prize of the high calling of God in Christ Jesus.

Shortly after my brother died in May of 1996, Granny Lucy developed another bout of cancer and refused to have any more surgeries. With the sudden loss of my brother, she grieved for his loving presence. She had developed survivor's grief and felt it should have been her, not her young grandson! So, she made up her mind to go back to her homeland of Trinidad. She told me that she loved me and that the next time we would meet again would be in heaven. I hugged and kissed her and didn't want to let her go. She died from cancer within the month.

My fondest memory of my granny was her receiving salvation through my brother's six-month ministry of evangelism. I remember coming home from college one day during the week. Walking through the front door, I saw an image of Granny and Sheldon, an image now imprinted in my memory forever. My brother was kneeling by her bedside, and her

---

[1] https://www.christianity.com/bible/msg/genesis/5-24 - Matthew Henry's Commentary on Genesis 5:21-24.

hands were lifted. Tears were flowing like a flood from her eyes. She was calling out to the Lord to save her and forgive her sins. My grandmother kept reaching her hands up in the air as if to reach the hand of God. Finally, Granny was saved, set free, and redeemed into the Lamb's Book of Life. I will always treasure this memory because they are no longer with me. But thanks be to God, I will see them both again one day!

Life Lessons learned along the way....

I encourage you not to wonder if your loved ones are saved. It is imperative to ask God to allow you to witness to your family and share God's agape (forgiving and faultless) love with them. More than just saying it, they need to see it as being fixed and unconditional in our responses to them. I've learned that many family members will not read the Bible, but they will read your life and take notes. God's love does not waver for us when we mess up. He still sees us as the righteousness of God because He is righteous, and we are His children.

PRAYER: *Thank you, Father God, for teaching us to love our families without judging their walk. Help us to show our families how much you love them by watching our walk with You.*

I.

An Intruder

For I know the thoughts that I think toward you, saith the Lord, thoughts of peace, and not of evil, to give you an expected end. Jeremiah 29:11 (KJV)

In the year of Y2K, when everything computerized was supposed to shut down and not work, the devil tried to kill me, but my heavenly Father rebooted me! On September 21st, 2000, Jeremiah 29:11, as previously noted, became gut-real to my innermost being. This scripture was no longer just words written on a page in black and white in an old worn-out Bible. It was now the living word of God jumping off the page into my life. I saw with my own eyes and felt in my own body how the power of God could sustain you during a trial or test. Since surrendering my life to Jesus, I have experienced many spiritual battles. Sometimes I was prepared for them. Sometimes I was not. In this case, I can honestly say that, in hindsight, God prepared me for this appointed meeting with an intruder!

Often, after we become believers, God has a set time to grow and mature us. He allows us to undergo spiritual challenges that increase our fortitude and stamina. It is not to defeat us but to make us stronger in Him! We, as saints, are a lot stronger than we think. The testimony comes after you have undergone fiery trials, and you survive to give God all the glory!

I can recall being 25 years old, waking up one day, and going to work at the bank. After my brother died, I changed from working part-time to full-time to help support my family. I stayed at this job because it offered full benefits and tuition reimbursement while I went to school part-time. Like any other day of the week, after getting off work, I headed straight to school. I was studying to be an accountant. What for, I don't know. But I was too deep into my course loads to change majors as I was now in my third year. I told myself to stick it out and not quit.

After school, I remembered there was a women's conference at a local church I wanted to attend and headed over thereafter. I wanted to thank God for all the great things he was doing in my life! I knew God was with me, but I wish I had learned to listen and obey the unctioning (inner prompting to move) of the Holy Ghost[2] more fully. My stomach started doing somersaults, making me feel uneasy. I thought it was because it was evening and I had not eaten much that day. But it was quite the contrary. My inner man, the spirit of God inside each believer, warned

---

[2] The Holy Ghost, or Holy Spirit, is the third person of the Trinity in the Christian faith. He is a person, co-equal with God the Father and Jesus Christ, the Son.

me to turn around, but I was too young in the faith to realize that I was in danger!

I reached the top of my apartment stairs around 9:35 pm and put my key in my door. But to my horrific shock, it didn't work because the door lock had been broken and tampered with. My heart sank as I saw shavings from the door lock fall to the floor at my feet. Because of the weight of my work bag, school bag, umbrella, and purse all around my shoulders, I could not run, even though I attempted to. This is when I saw a big, black man's hand reach for my hair and pull me into my apartment. I quickly turned to try and run, but it was too late! I was caught off-guard, and he was too quick! Instinct caused me to fight back against this intruder trespassing in my home. We began to struggle. He was too strong for me! He hit me with the 38-caliber gun and threw me to the ground. When I came to, I had a gun cocked on the bridge of my nose and between my eyes!

Trying to get my bearings, I kept thinking silently, subconsciously trying to process all that was occurring. "Is this happening to me right now?" My worst nightmare was standing before me! This intruder was very upset and started using profanity in the worst way. He called me every hateful curse word that could roll off his tongue. Finally, he called me crazy for fighting back because he had a gun on me. When he finally calmed down, he began to give me instructions.

I was told to get up and not to look at his face. He had a white towel over his head, covering his whole face, and I could not see anything else about him. He took my umbrella from me, pushed me over to my couch, and told me to sit down with my hands in the air. Everything was moving so fast. I submitted temporarily to what this intruder wanted me to do because I did not know his intentions. Then, to increase his anxiety, my house phone rang. He started freaking out and wanted to know who was calling me. I told him that I did not know. He gave me instructions to call them back, and if I sounded like I was not convincing enough, he would blow my brains out while talking on the phone. So, with this 38-caliber gun stuck to my head, I made the call in a calm voice with the help of the Lord. I told the person who called I was okay and thanked them for checking on me. How can I explain that? As nervous as I was, I also had a calm and peace all over me. I can only say that it was the presence of God that I found in the scripture I knew by heart. John 14:27 (AMP):

> *Peace I leave with you; My [perfect] peace I give to you; not as the world gives do I give to you. Do not let your heart be troubled, nor let it be afraid. [Let My perfect peace calm you in every circumstance and provide you with courage and strength for every challenge.]*

Part of me wanted to cry out for help over the phone, but I quickly remembered I was being held at gunpoint! Convinced of my obedience, the intruder uncocked the gun from my head and pushed me back to my couch with my hands in the air. For a brief second, sitting there, I could hear a police car driving by. I was praying and hoping that someone saw something and reported it. But as I waited, the sound of the siren became fainter in the distance. So many thoughts then began rushing through my head. How did I get into this situation I'm in right now? How am I going to get out? Why did this intruder break into my apartment, and what did he want? I began to think... Lord, I need your help right now. Please show up and help me!

Life Lessons learned along the way....

This is why young men and women must read God's word and attend Bible Study regularly. Studying God's word allows you to learn His character and voice. Learn to listen to the unction of the Holy Ghost when He "warns" you not to go to certain places because there may be a danger. Don't discount that God speaks to you and will show His love and care for you. You will come to know His voice when He speaks to you because it will be followed by peace after you obey.

On the other hand, if you don't obey, you will feel troubled in your spirit for not following the instructions. This is an area of growth in every Christian's life. Your level of discernment to know God's voice or His Spirit increases as your relationship with God strengthens.

PRAYER: Father God, please help me to meditate on your word daily so that I can learn your voice and receive instructions from you. You said in the scripture John 10:27-29 (KJV),

My sheep hear my voice, and I know them, and they follow me: [28] And I give unto them eternal life; and they shall never perish, neither shall any man pluck them out of my hand. [29] My Father, which gave them me, is greater than all; and no man is able to pluck them out of my Father's hand.

And because I know your voice, Lord, I trust what you speak to me and won't doubt the direction in which you lead my life. Therefore, I am secure in Your hands.

My Faith is Being Tested

By: Shelena A. Hickman

My faith is being tested, Lord!

I am calling out to you!

Do you hear me, Lord?

I really don't know what to do!

I'm in a difficult situation.

I cry out with my hands lifted high!

Do you see me, Lord?

Please come quickly, come nigh!

You are here with me, Lord.

I feel your presence close!

Show me what to do, Lord!

Please help me, Holy Ghost!

II.

A Witness

Looking unto Jesus, the author and finisher of our faith, who for the joy that was set before Him endured the cross, despising the shame, and has sat down at the right hand of the throne of God. Hebrews 12:2 (NKJV)

Out of nowhere, this intruder began bragging about how good of a shooter he was and that he could shoot me with his right or left hand! As a result, my subconscious was starting to come alive because I was tired of sitting on my couch with my hands in the air, with someone throwing darts of profanity in my ears. I was getting angry about how this intruder was talking to me. He didn't even know me. How could he treat me this way? These were all the thoughts running through my head at the time. As the intruder spoke, his voice became faint in my ears because I was now facing this situation as a reality. I felt like I was in a fictional story, watching a drama unfold, but the very sound of his voice brought me back. I was being held at gunpoint for no reason from my perspective. I needed clarity to keep my mind sound. I began calling on the Lord from the inside of me. As I focused on tuning out this intruder, I started to feel the presence of my Heavenly Father. I was in a safe place. It felt like a bubble or a capsule where I was protected from anything and everything. It was a silent place. It was a serene place. It was a place full of peace separate from the outside of my body. I could no longer hear him cursing at me and calling me everything but a child of God.

I could sense the presence of God and began to tell Him how confused I was about my present circumstances. I remember crying on the inside, wanting to know if I had done something wrong to deserve this. I asked the Lord why He was doing this to me. I reminded him that I was living right and doing His will. As plain as I could hear the intruder in my living room speaking before entering this safe place with my Father, God answered me with another question. My Father in Heaven told me, "Shelena if this guy was to die tonight, where would his soul be? Where would he lift up his eyes?" The Lord then told me to witness to this lost soul. My eyes began to well up and fill with tears. The Lord showed me that I was never the victim in this situation because He had me in the palm of His hand, where no man could pluck me out of. I was no longer the victim in this situation. I belonged to the Father. John 10:28-30 (NKJV) declares it this way,

> *And I give them eternal life, and they shall never perish; neither shall anyone snatch them out of My hand. My Father, who has given them to Me, is greater than all; and no one is able to snatch them out of My Father's hand. My Father and I are one."*

After the Lord got my attention, I remember submitting to His will in my heart. I quickly resolved that if I died tonight, I would die doing the Lord's will because He knows His plans for me, and they were still thoughts of good, even though this did not look like a good situation. God was still good to me in this hellish moment of my life! So, I opened my mouth and began to witness to the intruder. I told him that Jesus loved him and that he did not have to live in sin. The more I said it, the stronger and bolder I felt. But, on the other hand, the intruder told me that he didn't want to hear about my Jesus and became angrier and angrier the more I said the name Jesus!

Being very hopeful, I prayed for a breakthrough with the intruder because I did what God asked me to do. But it was not working out that way. Contrary to my plan of salvation and repentance for this man, and a possible surrendering of his life to God, to my utter dismay, things shifted in the opposite direction. I was hoping that he would let me go unharmed. However, immediately after sharing the gospel of Jesus Christ with the intruder, he became so belligerent. The intruder spoke to me in a voice that scared me out of my wits concerning how he wanted to have some fun with me. He told me to take all my clothes off! I was horrified, but then a boldness arose in me! I started reflecting on all that had happened that evening and how late it was getting. It had been over an hour of me sitting on my couch. My hands were tired of being in the air and listening to this intruder cursing at me repeatedly!

This intruder did not know that I had vowed to God that no man would touch me unless I were married. This was a serious matter for me. Although I did not grow up knowing the scripture that said my body was the temple of the Holy

Spirit, it was an important commitment because God taught me how priceless my virginity was to Him. I was intentional about keeping my vessel clean for God's use. When I confessed my sins to the Lord and got saved, I knew God forgave me of all my sins and taught me in Bible Study how to live holy by the scripture. This scripture reference is found in I Corinthians 6:19-20 (NIV),

> *Do you not know that your bodies are temples of the Holy Spirit, who is in you, whom you have received from God? You are not your own; you were bought at a price. Therefore honor God with your bodies.*

And I was not going back on my word, even if it cost me my life! I told myself he would have to have fun with a corpse rather than invade this body that belonged to God! I saw my body as the temple of the Holy Ghost, and no one was going to defile it. So I knew that I had to make a move when he decided he wanted to rape me.

As I slowly got undressed, I was losing patience. Finally, my spirit switched to warfare mode, and I fought back! I knew my rights. This is my house. He is invading my territory. I began scanning my apartment for an object to use against him. As I bowed my head down to take off my shoes and pantyhose, I saw my coffee table a couple of steps before me. After I was down to my bra and underwear, I made my move. I tried to pick up my solid-oak coffee table to hit him with it, but it was too heavy. The adrenalin pumping in my mind was greater than the strength in my physical body! I dropped the table, and the glass shattered on me. I was so disappointed I could not lift it. I cried out to the Lord to help me. Then this man, possessed by a demon, stood over me and shot me at close range. The intruder shot me with a 38-caliber gun in the right temple of my brain and through my right breast.

The bullet hit my back rib cage and spiraled down to my right pelvis.

He then shot me in my left leg.

Every shot I tried to block went through my right wrist.

"My head, my head, my head!" is all I can remember repeatedly saying until I was somewhere watching a video of my mother and my two sisters still alive. The bullet to my head felt like a jackhammer constantly pounding. I don't recall feeling the other shots because the vibrations in my head took over all other senses and would not stop. I was barely hanging on. Then the sound suddenly stopped. I was lying on the floor - not in heaven or hell - but communing with my God in a peaceful place!

I asked the Lord if I could go and meet my brother Sheldon now. He told me plainly, "No! Get up. It is not your time yet. Get up and live!"

Immediately, I was alert and aware that I was in my apartment on the floor with gunshot wounds. I cannot remember how long I lay on the floor or of even being in pain when I woke up. I was mostly in shock and felt like this was not real and possibly a dream! But it all became a reality when I could physically hear that I was back in my apartment again. I was afraid to get up off the floor. So, the Lord told me to "listen," and that's when I heard my patio blinds blowing in the wind. Then, the Lord told me to get up because the intruder was gone over my balcony.

I Need a Witness

By: Shelena A. Hickman

I need a Witness

that will obey me

in the thick and the thin!

I need a Witness

that will obey me

and will surrender from within!

I need a Witness

that will obey me

and save a soul from sin!

Will you be that witness?

And so I did.

I got up, opened my apartment's front door, and began to run for help.

I started running down the street with a bullet in my leg,

a bullet in my chest,

an aneurysm to the brain,

and a bullet sticking out the right side of my brain!

I knew I was not alone because I was not feeling any pain!

Believe it or not, I was not in pain!

The adrenalin of the Lord and the caravan of angels I was calling on propelled me forward.

I felt so free. I did not know if I would leave my apartment alive.

But at that moment, being free and out of captivity felt good.

Whenever I think back to that time running, I see a picture of five-time Olympic sprinter, Marion Jones, running her best in the relay races that year. But, instead of running for a gold medal, I was running for my life!

While running to get help, I fell twice, running up and down stairs. After two unsuccessful attempts knocking at different doors in the apartment complex, I ran into a young man dressed in all white - hat, shirt, pants, and shoes. This man appeared as a beacon of light out of the darkness. Little did he know I was ready to give up hope of finding someone to help me until I ran into this godsend. He took me to see his wife in their apartment, and she covered me with a blanket to keep me warm. This kind-hearted lady then gave me some clothes to put on and spoke to me with care. Her husband called 911. While waiting, I saw myself in the dresser mirror for the first time since being shot. Seeing myself was not a good mental moment for me, especially when I saw the bullet sticking out with blood covering my head. This is when the trauma set in, and I got scared!

At that moment, I knew it was no longer a dream. It was a reality! I had just lived through a vicious attack from the enemy, and I was alive by the grace of God! "Who would do this, and why would they do this to me?" Those questions now started floating through my head. But I was not out of the woods yet.

Finally, the paramedics came. They initially had difficulty getting me out of the apartment because I thought the intruder was hiding in the bushes. Finally, they had to force me into the ambulance. I thought he was waiting to finish me off. But they were so kind. These angels took me on what seemed like the longest ride of my life to the hospital, comforting and attending to me the whole way. They took me to the Texas Medical Center, Memorial Hermann, in downtown Houston. I called them angels because I wanted to sleep, but they would not let me. Every time I felt myself falling asleep, I would hear someone talking to me to keep my eyes open. Of course, they knew, but I didn't realize then that I probably would not wake up again if I had fallen asleep!

But all praise be to God that caused me to triumph over my enemies! God had a plan because He gave me purpose!

After making it to the Emergency Room, I felt like I was in a holding pattern because I couldn't figure out why I was still lying on a table with bullets in my body, heated blankets on top of me, yet freezing cold! I remember hearing the doctors asking me whom they could call on my behalf in my family. I thought immediately of my Uncle Henry, and amazingly, by a miracle of God, I recalled his phone number from memory. The only problem was that he lived three hours away, and it would take a while for him to get there.

At this point, the plan of the Lord unfolded before my eyes. The well-known and respected doctor, Dr. James Henry "Red" Duke[3], who was either leaving or coming onto his shift, inquired about me lying on the hospital table. He was the next godsend God used to save my life. Because no one in my family knew I had been shot, they could not do the surgery without authorization. They needed someone to sign the necessary documents. Overhearing this discussion, I told the doctors that I was coherent. They questioned me several times by asking me my name, address, phone number, and social security number. After I answered all the questions with flying colors, with that bullet sticking out of my right temple, they decided I could sign up for the surgery. Over the

---

[3]   Dr. James Henry "Red" Duke (11/16/1928 – 08/25/2015). A renowned trauma surgeon who was instrumental in creating the Life Flight airlift program and hosted television health segments for 15 years. He was a trauma surgeon and professor at The University of Texas Health Science Center at Houston and Memorial Hermann-Texas Medical Center, where he worked on-site since 1972. He died from natural causes in 2015 at his beloved hospital at the age of 86.

next 24 hours, Dr. Duke and Dr. William Gormley worked to remove the bullets from my head and body.

I believe God anointed those two doctors to put me back together again. After waking up from surgery, I was surrounded by my family. I looked like a mummy, my head wrapped with white gauze and tubes flowing inside and outside me. My family assumed that I was in pain because I could not talk. They did not know that the tube inside my throat prevented my speech. So, when I discovered that I could move my arms, I started pointing to the tubes. When the tubes were removed, I was able to talk to my family. Tears flowed freely. I was so grateful to God for giving me life again. Because I trusted the Lord to heal my body and prayer warriors were praying for me, He expedited my healing process. My doctors agreed that I could be released from the hospital because they concluded nothing else was wrong with me. I just needed time for my body to heal from my life-saving surgery fully.

Before leaving the hospital, a physical therapist came to my room and taught me how to use a pillow to help me get out of a chair and bed without hurting myself. It took some time because my stomach muscles had to heal from the inside out. Finally, I was released from the hospital four days after multiple surgeries on my head and body! Praise God! Praise God! Praise God!

When I returned to see Dr. Duke and Dr. Gormley for my one-week follow-up, they were amazed at how quickly my head and stomach incisions had healed. My stomach and head looked like a patient that had surgery two months prior. The doctors confirmed no infection at any of the staples and that everything looked well. Dr. Duke declared me a living miracle! He marveled that I could stand after being shot in the right temple and run with an aneurysm to my brain! I am still here because He planted His purpose inside of me! I am here because there is a work God wants me to do for His kingdom! I remember running for my life to get help, and the scripture that kept flowing through my mind was 1 Thessalonians 5:18 (KJV),

> *In every thing, give thanks: for this is the will of God in Christ Jesus concerning you.*

So, while running for my life, with tears in my eyes, I began thanking God for His goodness. "*Thank you, Lord! I love you, Lord! Thank you, Lord! Even though I don't understand, I love you, Lord!*"

I genuinely believe that the spirit of praise on my lips unto God saved my life. I was giving God praise at a time when my mind and my body were being challenged, yet my inner spirit-man was not confused! I learned in Bible Study that I should always hide the Word of God in my heart so that it would come flowing out of me when I needed it to comfort me. John 7:38 (KJV) declares,

> I genuinely believe that the spirit of praise on my lips unto God saved my life.

> *He that believeth on me, as the scripture hath said, out of his belly shall flow rivers of living water.*

I thank God for my loving family and church family that called on other church families to pray and intercede for my life. Things could have turned out differently without their effective and fervent prayers bombarding heaven for me. Thank you, Jesus, for saving my life! I give you all the glory and all the praise in Jesus' name! Hallelujah!

Life Lessons Learned Along The Way...

Hindsight is very popular. Many people say that if they were in someone else's shoes, they would know what to do differently, but do we? All I can say is that your genuine relationship with God shows up when your faith is tested. You learn to understand Paul's testimony when he says in Philippians 1:21 (KJV),

For me, to live is Christ, and to die is gain.

Dying, as a result of living for Christ, for kingdom purposes, is the highest promotion.

I can honestly say that while being held at gunpoint, God revealed to me that He was always with me. I learned that whether I was promoted to heaven that night or lived to see another day, I was good because I had the victory! On the other hand, the intruder was afraid and tormented in his heart because he was in the wrong and out of the will of God. We have never found out who he is or why he attacked me. Nonetheless, even though he had evil intentions toward me, God touched my heart to share the message of salvation with him at a crucial moment of his life. Can we say that we would do the same if the tables of life were turned on us?

PRAYER: Father God, teach us how to see past what we are going through so that others may have a chance to come to the knowledge of you. Help us to have an effective witness! You said in 2 Peter 3:9 (AMP),

> *The Lord does not delay [as though He were unable to act] and is not slow about His promise, as some count slowness, but is [extraordinarily] patient toward you, not wishing for any to perish but for all to come to repentance.*

Remind us, Lord, that this life and earth are temporary, but you are an everlasting God that keeps His word for all eternity. Thank you for being our Waymaker and providing what we need in the midst of life's numerous storms.

My Provider

By: Shelena A. Hickman

God is taking care of me.

There is mistakenly no doubt!

When it looks like I'm down to nothing,

please don't count me out!

You see, I trust God

to show up and make a way!

It's not my load to carry

So I cry out to Him every day!

When I gave my life to Jesus,

I quickly learned on whom I could call!

So I say, Thank you, Jesus,

my Provider, in the midst of it all!

III.

God's Divine Plan

Trust in the Lord with all thine heart; and lean not unto thine own understanding. In all thy ways acknowledge him, and he shall direct thy paths. Proverbs 3:5-6 (KJV)

It had been three months since I left the hospital, and I knew I had some decisions to make. My Uncle Henry and Aunt Von did everything they could to help rehabilitate me, but I knew God was tugging on my heart. I was not going back to Baytown, where all this happened. God was telling me that it was time to return to Houston. I initially ignored that voice, but then it got stronger and louder! And on top of that, my Uncle Henry gave me an offer that made it hard to refuse, but I had to obey God!

My uncle offered me a rent-free place to stay with him while I went to school, all expenses covered. My only goal or focus would be to finish school. I loved my Uncle Henry because he was a positive father figure whom the Lord allowed to flow into my life in high school. He was the one that put the idea in my head that I could go to college and get a degree so that I could get a good-paying job. He was always encouraging me to be the best that I could be. Even though the offer was tempting, I kept hearing God say, "Are you going to trust me to take care of you again?" Because of the intruder, I intensely feared "young black men." Going back to Houston would make me face my fears one more time. The Lord asked me another question, "Who was in the apartment with you when you were in danger with a gun cocked to your head?" I kept telling Him that "It was you, Lord. It was you, only you!"

How do I recover what was lost when God temporarily allowed me to lose everything? I knew that God, my Father in Heaven, was leading me to face my fears. He wanted me to stand on II Timothy 1:7 (NKJV),

> *For God has not given us a spirit of fear, but of power, and of love, and of a sound mind.*

On the other hand, the enemy was trying to infiltrate me with lies, and if I went back to face my fears, I would be attacked again or even die this time! So, I had a decision to make. Was I going to believe the report of the Lord, who delivered me from the lion's den? Or was I going to believe the report of my adversary, the devil, that wanted to keep overwhelming me with paralytic fear, doubt, increased anxieties, and frustration about my future? Though hesitant, the answer was clear to me. Trust God with every part of my being, and He will lead and guide me because He knows what is best for me. My God has a convincing track record of deliverance and a mighty right hand of power! So, in January of 2001, I moved to Houston, Texas, and trusted God with my whole future because I knew God would be with me. I held Him to His word in Hebrews 13:5b (KJV), where the scripture says:

For He Himself has said, "I will never leave you nor forsake you."

Life Lessons Learned Along the Way...

We often give up too soon because we don't like the hand we're dealt in life. But if we learn to wait on the Lord and completely trust Him to lead and guide our future with no strings attached, He will reveal a purposeful life beyond comprehension.

Thank you, Lord, for trusting me to obey you in the lean and hard times when I didn't understand and thought I was too good to go through those trials. I had the misconception that I was exempt from bad things happening to me because I obeyed God. I believed that because I paid my tithes and offerings, read my Bible, attended Bible study and church, volunteered at the church, and kept my vessel pure from fornication, I would not have to endure any bad trials. Newsflash!!! When

> I was too good to go through those trials. I had the misconception that I was exempt from bad things happening to me because I obeyed God.

you are sold out in mind, body, soul, and spirit to God, He chooses how He will use you for His glory! Remember, you are the clay; He is the Potter, turning your life as He sees fit on His wheel. First, he allows the pressures of life to be turned up so that you can be refined in the fire. He then removes particles of matter that do not belong in your mind, heart, and soul. No matter the obstacle, the Lord wants His agape love to exude out of you! God wants you to rise above what has been attacking you!

PRAYER: *Father God, please take the steering wheel of my life. I do not have a clue as to what I am doing. Every time I try to fix it, I make it worse. At times, I feel like a child that needs constant reminders to stay on task. Keep me childlike in my faith but not childish in obeying Your will for my life. Please help me to move past the fork in the road where I still want to do it my way. Let me mean it for real when I say... Lord, I genuinely surrender all!*

Starting Over Again!

By: Shelena A. Hickman

I don't want to waste time looking back

on the way things used to be.

I just want to trust you, Lord,

and follow your constant lead.

It's sometimes hard

looking past where I am.

My heart longs to trust you all the way.

But my thoughts constantly waver,

focusing on the challenges I have to face.

Because I want to grow,

I will choose to speak life

and exercise my faith in your Word.

I know that you can deliver me

through every testimony that I've heard!

So, Lord, when you see me

holding my head down

because life's pressures have seeped in,

please gently remind me to look up.

as you walk with me,

Starting Over Again!

IV.

Window Of Opportunity

Brethren, I count not myself to have apprehended: but this one thing I do, forgetting those things which are behind, and reaching forth unto those things which are before, I press toward the mark for the prize of the high calling of God in Christ Jesus.
Philippians 3:13-14 (KJV)

Starting over was difficult mentally because I had to trust and depend on family members, my church family, and friends to help me make it for a season. I worked temporary jobs until the Lord allowed me to finish college. The Lord opened a window of opportunity for me to take 43-course hours in one year with encouragement from my Uncle Henry, Aunt Von, and my church family. While attending school in June of 2003, I received a call that my sister, Sherene, had died after suffering a seizure. She was just 23 years old. I took a week off from school to bury her, then went back and wrote my accounting paper and turned it in. This period of life was overwhelming for me. The pressures kept piling up in the midst of my pressing toward graduation. I strongly considered giving up!

This death of my second sibling hurt because I felt like God was picking on us as a family. My mom was already struggling with my brother's death and my attempted murder. We were all grieving for our loved ones in different ways. This would be the second body I would have to identify as my sibling in seven years. How do we recover from this one too? This loss was especially significant because I was helping my sister plan her wedding. Now I had to plan her funeral instead.

What do I say to her 2-year-old daughter, my niece? How do I comfort my sister Sharleen, the only sibling I have left? I could not afford to break down. So I kept reading my Bible, going to Bible study, and trusting God. I felt ashamed, as if my family was targeted for trials, but I kept serving God and declaring He was still good to me.

At the funeral, I had to encourage myself in the Lord. I could feel the conversations of the people talking about me and praying that I wouldn't lose it. I can honestly say that the power of prayer works and that God kept my mind! My mom has always been a praying woman, and I knew she was praying for all of us. A friend gave me a song on a CD, and I would play it repeatedly on my darkest days. The song was "You can make it!" by Betty Griffin Keller. It still ministers to me today.

I made it through the Summer of 2003. Then, September 2003 came, and my grandfather, Alfred Miller Guide, died. I loved my grandfather because he was another positive father figure in my childhood. I remember going to the grocery store with him and helping him work on cars in his garage. He would always buy me my favorite candy bar, *Whatchamacallit*, as a reward for helping him with the weekly groceries.

One month later, in October 2003, my great-grandmother, Ruby Senhouse, died at age 90. I have many fond memories of my great-granny, and I loved her. So, I began reflecting and thanking God for my childhood memories on the islands with her and for allowing me to see her on her birthday before she went to be with the Lord.

Life Lessons Learned Along the Way...

Whenever times get tough, I am reminded of my brother's encouragement. He would say, "Thank you, Lord, for showing me I am on the right track. Thank you, Lord, that my blessings are right around the corner." I've learned that I wouldn't know how resilient I was without opposition until I was tested! God is still good in every trial and every test, even though it doesn't feel good when you go through it.

Even though I experienced multiple trials the closer I got to my graduation, God made me a promise in Isaiah 43:2 (NLT),

When you go through deep waters and great trouble, I will be with you. When you go

*through rivers of difficulty, you will not drown!
When you walk through the fire of oppression,
you will not be burned up—the flames will
not consume you.*

PRAYER: Father God, thank you for every test, trial, opposition, attack, every no, every door closing, job loss, failure, death, disappointment, lack of supplies, and every attack that came against your Word. Through Your guidance, I can see how you were with me even in the darkest moments of my life. Thank you for never leaving me there but always finding ways to increase my hope in You and Your Word. Because of your plans for my life, I am victorious no matter what obstacles I face. Thank you for being there for me when I needed you most.

Window of Opportunity

By: Shelena A. Hickman

I've opened for you a window

it's available for you to reach.

At times it may seem impossible,

but I encourage you to seek.

I've given you an opportunity

to be all that you can be.

Many may try to persuade you otherwise,

but I have purposed for you to succeed!

You've been set apart,

not by your smarts and abilities.

But because I've chosen you

to excel both spiritually and intellectually.

So, get ready and take flight,

for I have equipped you to achieve.

It will not be by your power or your might.

For I am your Heavenly Father,

granting you this blessed

Window of Opportunity!

V.

My God Did It!

Trust in the Lord with all thine heart; and lean not unto thine own understanding. In all thy ways acknowledge him, and he shall direct thy paths. Proverbs 3:5-6 (KJV)

What the devil meant for evil, God worked it out for my good! He used all my challenges in 2003 to show me how strong I was. Because I returned to Houston and trusted God to lead and guide my future, I graduated in December 2003 with a Bachelor's Degree in Accounting and a 3.00 GPA. All praise, honor, and glory goes to my God in Heaven! The miracle of this celebration was that God allowed me to accomplish this after being shot in the head! So, my complete testimony is that God did it! I obeyed His voice, and He worked a miracle through me. He confirmed to me in Philippians 4:13 (ERV) that,

> *Christ is the one who gives me the strength I need to do whatever I must do.*

God has been guiding me all along, and I am sharing this testimony because all the glory belongs to Him.

Most assuredly, I have grown in my love walk with the Lord. I never took the time to hate the intruder that shot me. Instead, I felt sorry for him, and the Lord told me to pray for him. I believed that my obedience to pray for him was why I never felt ill toward him. He was a sinner who needed a Savior, and God sent him my way to give him another chance.

> My choice to forgive him for disrupting my life was a "must" for me to move forward.

I could not wait for an apology from the intruder who shot and hurt me. I had to move on with my life. I don't know if he is saved or dead now, but I know that my choice to forgive him for disrupting my life was a "must" for me to move forward. I decided I wanted all God had for my future, and hating this man would only rob me of moving on. In Mark 11:25-26 (AMP), the scripture says,

Whenever you stand praying, if you have anything against anyone, forgive him [drop the issue, let it go], so that your Father who is in heaven will also forgive you your transgressions and wrongdoings [against Him and others]. [But if you do not forgive, neither will your Father in heaven forgive your transgressions."]

48

Life Lessons Learned Along the Way...

The obedient act of forgiveness is for you, not for the person you are at odds with! Freedom comes when you release your oppressors to God and allow Him to handle the situation. Sometimes God allows the heat of the furnace to flare up so that He can remove hidden sins in our hearts. If you have difficulty forgiving someone for something they did in your childhood, it's time to stop and think. If innocent Jesus could bear the cross for my sins and He did nothing wrong, how much more can I find in my heart to forgive? So it's time to release the person(s) that have hurt you, whether they know it or not, and move forward in God's glorious plans for your life!

PRAYER: Father God, I have to be honest and tell you that I am struggling with forgiveness. I know it is the right thing to do, but the very thought of what the person(s) did, troubles me. Father, just like you blotted out my transgressions when I asked for forgiveness, take the memory of the pain away from my mind, heart, and emotions. I make a conscious decision today that I will not hold anyone hostage in my mind because the only prisoner I'm hurting is me. So, I decree and declare John 8:36 (NKJV) over my life right now in Jesus' name. *Therefore, if the Son makes you free, you shall be free indeed.* AMEN

My God Did It!

By: Shelena A. Hickman

I traveled many miles

through sunny days and rainy days

often filled with pain.

I had to face many challenges,

that would have caused many to give up,

and not want to try again.

There were times

that the enemy tried to convince me,

it was much better just to quit.

—Saying, "Serving with a thorn, you cannot do it!"

But thanks be to God,

I can now testify, encourage

and tell others in the faith:

"I did not accomplish this task on my own.

I was guided by my "Daddy" in heaven above,

To whom I owe all the credit.

"Yes, oh Yes…. *My God did it!*"

VI.

My Life Has Purpose

Being confident of this very thing, that he which hath begun a good work in you will perform it until the day of Jesus Christ. Philippians 1:6 (KJV)

It has been 23 years since this incident happened to me on September 21, 2000. I can most definitely say that God, my heavenly Father, my Daddy, has been with me the whole time. He has led and guided my life into the freedom I am walking in today.

The Lord told me it was now time to share this testimony so that others may know that the power of the Living God is still at work in his vessels of life today. He wants you to know that He is not partial to any one person, and what He did for me through my obedience to Him is what He wants to offer you today—no, not being shot three times and left for dead in your apartment. No! That's not what I am saying. I'm saying that the trials God allows to come your way are part of your development and spiritual growth. God does not create evil but allows it to manifest to show you how powerful He is in your life.

Today, I am no longer a victim of what I went through. I am a child of God, walking in victory because God loved me so much to save me when I cried out to Him. While going through my seasons of testing, I could not see the blessed future I am enjoying right now with my family. God showed me that He could restore the relationship with my earthly dad. And I can say I love my dad and thank God for the many laughs, talks, and prayers we pray together now. I am also glad that my mom lives with me and is living her best life today. She loves the Lord, and most of all, she looks nothing like what she has been through! Both of my parents love the Lord and are running the Christian race in such a way as to please the Lord with all their heart, mind, and soul. The Lord is increasing their latter days to be greater than their former. I treasure the relationship with my mom and dad even more.

I had to trust God by faith that my future would be brighter than it was then. Looking back, I can see God's hand on my life through every trial. His grace and mercy carried me through the toughest times of my life. God has given me purpose, and that's why I'm still here!

I still have a titanium plate holding my skull together with screws, a bullet lodged in my right pelvis, and a bullet floating around in my left leg today, but I am so grateful to God for sparing my life! He saw fit to bring me back with all my faculties and full movement of my limbs. It is because of my God, Jehovah Rapha, my healer, that I am restored and made whole! So, I declare Acts 17:28a (KJV) over my life,

For in him we live, and move, and have our being,

Thank you, Lord, for counting me worthy to go through for your glory in Jesus' name.

SO BE IT! Amen!

Life Lessons Learned along the way...

Quite simply put, I thank God that there was purpose in the pain! Sometimes as believers, we face multiple trial-attacks, hitting us from all different directions. The trials become so intense that we can't and don't see the benefits while we're in it. For a season, it seems like we are the only ones going through, and it appears as if we are not going to make it. But if we hold on to our Heavenly Father's hand and don't give up, there is a bright light of shining hope at the end. For this reason, God allows us to go through diverse storms so that we can comfort those in need. According to 2nd Corinthians 1:3-4 KJV,

3 Blessed be God, even the Father of our Lord Jesus Christ, the Father of mercies, and the God of all comfort; 4 Who comforteth us in all our tribulation, that we may be able to comfort them which are in any trouble, by the comfort wherewith we ourselves are comforted of God.

PRAYER: Father God, I want to thank you for every test that You allowed to come my way. I receive Your purpose for my life, and I will use every testimony that you have given me to comfort Your people in their times of need. You will always get all of the glory from my life because I belong to You, and the plans You have for my life are good! Hallelujah Amen!

God Had a Plan

By: Shelena A. Hickman

You took me to a lonely place

and told me, "Seek my face."

As much as it hurt inside,

I obeyed your will

and quickly, I began to abide.

You stripped me and primed me

down to my very core.

Pulling me away from family and friends,

I didn't think I could take much more!

I would have given up

and missed out on my many blessings.

Thank you for giving me strength

in all my seasons of testing!

Looking back now, Lord,

I can see how you led me

with your righteous right hand.

Not an experience was ever wasted!

My God, You had a Plan!

VII.

Salvation and Restoration Are Free For The Asking

The Word that saves is right here, as near as the tongue in your mouth, as close as the heart in your chest.
Romans 10:8 (MSG)

God's teaching is near you; it is in your mouth and in your heart. Romans 10:8 (ERV)

It is the teaching of faith that we tell people. If you openly say, "Jesus is Lord," and believe in your heart that God raised him from death, you will be saved. Yes, we believe in Jesus deep in our hearts, and so we are made right with God. And we openly say that we believe in Him, and so we are saved.

Restore Me, Oh Lord!

By: Shelena A. Hickman

Restore Me, Oh Lord,

before I draw further from you.

Restore me, Oh Lord,

for my inner man longs to be renewed.

Help me to look at my present situation

as a faith walker of what's to be;

not looking back and focusing

on the many disappointments I see.

Grant me your grace and endurance;

instead of running from the trial that you have set.

Show me the way of hope, Oh Lord,

for you have never failed me yet!

So, rebuild me, Oh Lord,

for I know your Word is true.

Restore me, Oh Lord,

for I now see Heaven in my view!

I choose to look up to you, Oh Lord since my soul has
been refreshed.

How can I forget your unselfish acts of love

when you sacrificed your son…

Jesus Christ, your best!

In Appreciation

Thank you for taking the time to read my testimony. I pray that the miracles shared in this book increase your faith to know that Jesus is real! He wants a relationship with you. Don't fight the process! Allow Him to prune you; you will be sanctified and made whole for the Master's use. We are the clay, and He is the Potter. We are the vines, and He is the Vinedresser. Trust God and ask Him to show you your purpose in life. Then, as the Lord leads you, please share this testimony with your family and friends so they, too, can know and experience the Power of God in their lives today!

God Bless You,

Shelena A. Hickman

About the Author

First, I am a child of God, saved by much grace! The testimony you are about to read will show the power of God and that He still performs miracles for His children. Second, I am living today because God delivered me from being held at gunpoint for about 1 hour in my apartment by an intruder. Third, this book will reveal how much the Heavenly Father desires no man to perish and the unconditional agape love He has to reach the lost. Even though the details may seem like scenes out of a movie, they are not! Each part of this testimony really happened, and I am living to give God the glory for saving me from an untimely death. I pray that this testament of God's sovereign power will draw you to a closer walk with your Heavenly Father. Whether you need salvation or restoration to believe again, I declare this book will inspire you to seek God like you never have before!

I am the wife of a fantastic husband, the mother of a miracle son, a bonus daughter, and the Nana of three grandchildren. During the day, I am a full-time Math teacher. At night, I am the Pen of a Ready Writer for God's glory!

Please comment on how this book blessed you or increased your faith and send it to: **penrw451@gmail.com.**